HER Silence Broken

Inspiration & Poetry

Yoshara S. Barber

HER Silence Broken

Copyright © 2018 by Yoshara S. Barber

All rights reserved. No part of this book may be reproduced or transmitted in any form or by any means without written permission of the author.

ISBN 978-0-692-06612-6

Contents

Breaking Silence - Introduction 1
The Silence She Kept 3
HER Abuse 5
The Cries from Within 8
HER Loneliness 11
Honestly Broken 14
HER Miscarriage 17
The Realness of the Illness 20
HER Defeats 23
Rebirthed 25
HER Reawakening 27
Prison of Peace 30
HER Choices 33
Shadow of Emotions 36
Why HER 39
Ultimate Sacrifices 41
HER Sacrifice 45

Rejection was the Set Up 47
HER Rejections 51
Embedded Fears 53
HER Fears 55
When Broken Became Repaired 57
HER Healing 59
For Better or For Growth 61
HER Growth toward Progressing 63
I Choose ME 65
HER Self-worth 67
Dancing Through 71
HER Breakthrough 73
United We Stand 75
HER Leadership 79
HER Silence Broken (The Voice Within) - Epilogue 83

About the Author 87

Breaking Silence

I took all the bricks thrown at me and created a stepping stone. I overcame obstacles by choosing not to run around the hurdles placed before me, but by a willingness to challenge myself. Instead of crawling, crying, or lying still, I inadvertently chose to dance through my troubles. I broke through the silence of brokenness that kept me so bound because I had an earnest expectation that greater was ahead.

How do we begin to dissect ways to break the silence that has held us so captive? Those feelings of incomplete, loneliness, rejections, and disappointments. The subtle feelings of emptiness, brokenness, and feelings of defeat. And how do we begin to conquer ways to learn how to challenge our inner fears in an effort toward reaching our full potential and gaining success?

I can almost guarantee you this process won't be easy. In fact, it will be one of the most difficult challenges you've ever had to face in life. It takes a lot to admit being honestly broken. It takes even more to accept yourself and to face yourself—the real you—in the mirror daily. I'm not talking about the person you pretend to be for the likes on social media, the cameras, or for the job. I'm referencing the person who is hidden inside of you, the person who is broken. That individual who is pushing their way through life's struggles, but hanging on by a thread in hopes of not breaking. That individual who has dealt with so much rejection and carries abandonment issues that in loving the wrong person several times has now caused them to be afraid to love at all.

We are our worst critics and accepting the weight of who we are can be difficult. At times it requires revealing our truths, focusing on removing the veil, and healing the open wounds that are apparent in our lives. The goal is working to build our self-esteem and self-confidence in a way that allows us to be okay with what happened, because what happened doesn't necessarily define what can happen. You see, we distract ourselves from our truths because we are so caught up in what we feel instead of realizing our truths can be used to help someone else's situation. We often become so wrapped up in pretending because we are afraid of who others see us as. We have a plan but no purpose.

But new places and new stages meant learning to confront her truth. Travel this journey of hope with her to focus on real-life issues. Daily issues that both men and women experience but hold inside because the thought of allowing others to see the scars, which are imprinted on them, seems all too damaging. She learned how to get to a place of forgiving those who had hurt her through self-talks and inspirations, in hopes of receiving something much greater.

The Silence She Kept

Black families are the worst when it comes to hiding our scars.
Hidden traumas of anger, relived memoirs,
Why was it so hard to trust someone with her truths?
Opening up to be rejected, pains that affected her youth.
Molestation, incest, rape to name a few,
This silence that she held inside she didn't know what to do.

Ashamed of being taking advantage for a lack of better gain.
Abandonment issues took place, it was driving her insane.
She ran to a person she thought would understand, just to be shut down.
She lost control of everything, she felt so let down.
Lack of understanding of what rape really was,
I thought he really loved me or was this just because
Because he wanted to hurt me or did he have an addiction?

Addiction to pain and young girls to where I felt conviction.
This silence she kept soon affected the men she would date.
Rejected in every aspect believing it was too late,
Too late to remove the hurt of brokenness that took over her mind.
Daddy issues that caused her to fall for a man that was kind.
Kind to her body but it was nothing more.
Satisfying his cravings as he had done before.

Visuals and beliefs that that was all men wanted.
Raised insecurities when issues were confronted.
So what do you do when the innocence of your youth is taken?
When there's no order of protection so instead you feel forsaken.

Yoshara S. Barber

How do we live with the ones who vowed to cover us?
That despite the abuse I held within, the truth was defined as mistrusts.
Distrustful of knowledge, was this what they called love?
Unknowingly lost, feeling neglectful.

Broken silence rendered the heart.
Meaningful regrets ready for a new start.
A chance to reveal this truth that was so real.
Empathetic emotions too sensitive to heal.

"Don't judge yourself by what others did to you."
C. Kennedy, Ómorp

HER Abuse

How do you handle when others know parts of you that you kept silent? Significant parts of you that allow others to see you for *you*. To see why you reacted to certain situations the way you did or why you held up so many guards. How do you begin to challenge the issues that affected you at youth, and how do you begin to move forward even while loneliness is attacking you at every angle?

For many years she fought to get to this place. Her truths were hidden. She was in a constant mind battle of what she believed because of what she told herself over the years. You see, the moment we have our truths revealed, instead of confronting it, we act as if nothing happened. Instead of pretending, we choose to run from the problem as opposed to facing them. We often look for what's going to cover us up. And like so many, she did the same.

What do you do when someone finds out something you have buried? Many times we continue to run to the next phase of our lives because we don't want others to see us. We begin to wear masks and put on designer clothing, and often speak a certain way all to cover up the reality of what it is we're choosing not to face. Handling when others know parts of you that you kept secret can be difficult. It is difficult in that many times when you are ready to reveal such things, you open yourself up to be judged, and oftentimes, people would rather judge you for the way you handled the situation based upon their perspectives. Opening up to anyone about an abuse is difficult, but understanding the risks of holding it in can be detrimental to your physical and emotional health as well. Without help (and even with help), sexual abuse has many difficult and harmful consequences. There is physical pain, emotional pain, confusing fears, isolation, shame, loss of trust, and possible guilt about the situation. Many children and youth, who have suffered from sexual abuse, can often grow up with low self-esteem, confusing angers and fears, unhappiness, depression, and relationship challenges. Often, sexual abuse of any kind is so confusing and awful that the child or youth goes into shock and cannot remember what happened, even for decades. Abused children and youth can often live in their own world completely "forgetting" the abuse, even as it's happening. Without help, many victims of sexual abuse may constantly need confirmation about who they really are throughout their lives and without effective assistance, successful adult relationships can be extremely difficult. The effects on the child or youth of being sexually abused can be complicated by any number of factors, including effects of abandonment and rejection issues.

It is extremely important for parents to understand the signs of sexual abuse. Learning the signs and how to speak with your child before anything happens is equally important. If your child has been abused, seek professional help for yourself so that you can be considerate and effective in your support for your child. Being supportive is the best thing you can be for your child. Take effective action because painful consequences of sexual abuse will continue emerging.

Lastly, remember it takes time. Do not rush the healing process. Be accepting, understanding, and patient. It took her several attempts to get to this point of healing. Not verbalizing such things to the authority figures in her life for fear of being judged was what allowed her to hold these things inside. Do not hold on to the abuse of what happened in your life. Realize who you can talk to for support and comfort in order to heal.

The Cries from Within

Tales of emptiness took over her mind
Loneliness crippled the heart that was blind.
Blind to love and lovers quarrels
Abandonment issues forgetful of morals.

Lost in the silence of others voices
Pretending to be okay despite her choices.
Holding the pain in to get through the day
Keeping her head up, knowing everything would be okay.

Smiling within because she was that much closer
She knew in her heart that it wasn't over.
Fighting through obstacles, breaking down barriers
Learning to trust despite the terror.

Troubles of past darkness working toward defeat
Prayers to high places that wouldn't leave her incomplete.
Trying to change, adapt to a world of adversities
Learning to adjust despite the uncertainties.

Cries in the darkness are held within
Another day to conquer this world we live in.
Waiting for happiness to greet her at the door
Stumbling upon strength in hopes of evermore.

Evermore gladness instead of sadness
Reducing the speed of pain that drove her to madness.
Sunshines of blessings that caused her to heal
Silent tears that no one should feel.

HER Silence Broken

She cried from within
I hope I won't have to wait to heal.
Until you feel as broken as I feel,
Waiting to find something that is real
Knowing this journey was all too surreal.

> "I'm lonely. And I'm lonely in some horribly deep way and for a flash of an instant, I can see just how lonely and how deep this feeling runs. And it scares the shit out of me to be this lonely because it seems catastrophic."
> Augusten Burroughs

HER Loneliness

Alone is lonely. That's what she remembers telling herself. How was she trapped in a world where she constantly felt like all she had was herself? Why did she feel so alone in a world surrounded by millions of people? Was she guilty? Was she unloved, unwanted? Or was it that she felt misunderstood? Maybe it was just a battle between herself and her own thoughts. Her mind told her for sure that she was alone, though. She desperately craved a connection from others and longed for specific experiences, and she wanted so badly for people to satisfy them. Yet somehow she inadvertently isolated herself in the process. For whatever reasons, at the end of it all, she knew how it felt. And that was broken and alone.

Everyone at some point in their lives has dealt with feelings of inadequacies and abandonment issues. Maybe it was something in your childhood that triggered it or reminded you of painful memories and why you felt like an outcast. She was her. What many did not know was the many obstacles she faced over the years, which were the result of the strength she had shown. How for so many years she had conjured up a way to appear happy, courageous, and exemplify strength, because she was afraid of portraying weakness in front of others. Many did not know her story at all. They did not understand the reasonings of how her struggles had somehow strengthened her faith.

How Prayer Worked in Her Life

For it took her many years to grow into the person that others saw her as. Sometimes she felt that others often pushed her into a light that she did not believe was capable of shining in her life. It appeared that she had merely confirmed leaving behind what she believed to be painful childhood experiences and rather choosing to channel her inner fears. She chose knowingly to smile in the face of adversity. But little did most know, this journey had not been so easy.

You see, the first part of her problem was that she had communication issues. She was very good at listening to others and many came to her for advice, and she was even good at writing how she felt about others and about herself. But the one thing she struggled with was effectively communicating her feelings to others. She had to learn how to communicate to people that she felt this way because someone had done this or she reacted this way because they made her feel this way in order to reach a deeper solution. Instead of facing the challenges head on and identifying a solution in an honest and appropriate way, she knowingly chose to avoid conflict and that meant avoiding the issues all together, even if that meant not talking and shutting down.

A lot of times, loneliness happens because it's a state of mind. It's what we are constantly telling ourselves. It's our beliefs that we create in our minds, and usually it is what naturally happens. So what is the best solution for this? What you can begin to do is change who you are connected with. I'm not saying that you have to totally cut people off. What I am saying is that you simply learn to adjust. Oftentimes our family and friends aren't being unsupportive but merely offering what they could at their capacity. Instead of choosing to fault them for it, simply refocus your attention and energy to those who are supportive, and those are the people to choose to stay closely connected to and rely on in the future. As time progressed, she began to speak to those she was closely connected to at work about goals and future aspirations for motivation and encouragement, and it became quite beneficial. Refocus your mindset and build your own support system. Build a support system of people who support you in terms of maintaining a commitment. You need someone to stay closely connected with. Someone who you can rely on for support and encouragement, especially while trying to break the silence of loneliness that's been keeping you so down.

Life is a series of lessons with a lot of uncertainties. The more she experienced and explored her own feelings of uncertainty and loneliness, the more she realized how necessary those feelings were. It's good for us to spend time exploring unknowns alone, however, make sure you are leaving room to alleviate certain issues and not causing yourself to pull away and become withdrawn.

Honestly Broken

Brokenness is a term few care to admit
The act of showing vulnerability is something we'd rather resist.
Opening ourselves to admit we are hurting
Revealing our truths bares room for uncovering.
Uncovering the veil of what really lies beneath
Beneath the scars of emptiness, shame, and defeat.

How can one feel loved when they're continuously rejected?
When no matter how hard they've fought to belong
They would rather be disconnected.
Disconnected from a world in which they're judged for poor choices
But whose to say those choices weren't valid?
A decision that left them feeling voiceless.

Can you imagine the individual who is drowning in defeat?
The lack of self-confidence is something they fail to meet.
I can't imagine the person who is ready to let go
That despite their current circumstances no one would even show.
Show them what it was like to break down a wall
Show them that the weight of who they were was worth it all.

What if being honestly broken meant revealing my truths?
The scars, the rapes, the turmoil, the physical and emotional abuse.
What if at the risk of being honestly broken,
It meant depending on the very people who hurt me?
That in spite of the lesson it showed me, it deferred me.
Or what if they never apologize for how they hurt me?
Lord, are you really asking me to take a knee to pray despite my tragedy?

HER Silence Broken

You see, to no degree she had to see,
What it was like to be set free.
Free from pain, free from struggling,
Free from a world that brought much suffering.
But she knew she wasn't free from it all
In fact, this was a much bigger call.
A reflection of a generational curse that needed broken

A young woman still learning to be outspoken.
So what if at the cost of your destiny, it demands vulnerability?
It demands the fears that we hide within; it demands releasing hostility.
Being honestly broken meant uncovering the truth, but this time with pride
It meant being transparent enough to admit it happened,
But I'm willing to set it aside.

For my destiny I'm willing to forgive,
And for my children I was willing to heal,
Because being honestly broken meant still being able to live.
That this pain I held so deep within
Could not stop how I was ready to begin.
Begin this new chapter of SELF-love
Self-realizations, self-affirmations of what was yet to come,
Aborting pain and agony in hopes of birthing greater outcomes.
You see, the distance between the reality of where I was and where I'd hoped to be seemed like an eternity,
I had to allow destiny to be fueled so big inside of me that it would break down the areas of brokenness.
I was willing to close my eyes for a second and get honest about my dreams,

And then I was willing to reopen my eyes to get honest about my truths.
I had an understanding that my purpose was somehow worth the pain,
That he who was out to save me had no room for shame.

So I say, don't worry about where you are right now,
Realize you just had a bad start
That the reality of where you are headed has everything to do with
    your heart.
Get honest about yourself and goals to produce a healthier life
Worry less, pray more, even if nothing will ever suffice.
Keep pushing yourself toward your destiny,
Keep building your self-confidence
Regardless how big the consequence, you didn't allow it to ruin your
    consciousness.
It is in our failures in which we succeed,
Although the light at the end of the tunnel makes it hard to believe,
But breathe it, sense it, believe it, feel it and
Understand that the lesson carried a weight that was so great
That you had to hurt to earn it.

"It has been said, 'time heals all wounds.' I do not agree. The wounds remain. In time, the mind protecting its sanity covers them with scar tissue and the pain lessens. But it is never gone."
Rose Kennedy

HER Miscarriage

A miscarriage, known in medical jargon as a spontaneous abortion, is the unexpected end of something that was supposed to be birthed. It is one of those topics that few people like to discuss, whereas it renders pain and agony. It brings about a sense of self-doubt that your mind doesn't seem capable of handling. You feel defeated because your body is having difficulty carrying this said weight and so now doubt presents itself. It's a lot similar to how our lives are operated each day.

Have you ever felt defeated because you set a particular goal for yourself and then life happened? Whether it was a job you were interested in and you were told someone else was more qualified; you allowed yourself to be this amazing girlfriend to someone for years, only to be told that they chose to marry someone else; or what about being a wife, who is dedicated and committed to her marriage, but at times feels unappreciated because all that you do goes unnoticed? The sacrifices you make allows you to feel as though you are existing in a world that revolves only around your family; a family you love, whom you just want to take an interest in the efforts you make. You have all these dreams and desires for which you have planned your life, but what happens when it doesn't go the way you planned? What do we do when we feel our destiny is miscarried?

We all want to become winners by being successful, but where we fail is that we don't understand what success looks like. We don't know how success feels in terms of seeing someone close to us succeed. So, what if your family is waiting to see what leadership looks like? What if they are waiting to see what being successful looks like, but at the cost of receiving success, you continuously fall short at the process and you are crying within? You find yourself breaking and in actuality you want to throw in the hand in which you were dealt. We want to choose who should have been our father, and who should have been our mother (or another boss) not realizing the process of your struggles and the reason you're dealt the hand you're dealt.

You see, your destiny has a provision for your ignorance, but what if at the cost of fulfilling your dreams, your destiny has to be miscarried? And what if during that process of miscarriage, it requires being evicted and having no transportation or even sustaining abuse? What if it requires admitting that you are honestly broken? What if it requires depending on the very people that hurt you or in spite of your forgiveness for them, what if they never apologize for how they treated you and how they hurt you?

You see, destiny demands vulnerability, and even when the odds are stacked against us, in order to be delivered, one must allow destiny to be fueled so big inside of them that it breaks down the areas of brokenness. She had to allow herself to become vulnerable in order to heal, and she had to allow herself to be vulnerable at the risk of her own destiny in order to become healthy, in order to become whole.

You see, we tell ourselves that we want better things that come with having successes, that come with reaching and obtaining our destiny, but the reality is we don't want the process it takes to achieve those successes. We don't want to abort something in hopes of birthing something even greater.

When you begin to run after your destiny, you will automatically run from your history. Believe that your scars have a lot less to do with where you've been and a lot more to do with where you're going. Don't be afraid of the stripes. Be afraid of staying the same. Be willing to take a few stripes and allow yourself to become uncomfortable at the cost of your destiny. Your destiny is important, but it's also important to remember the process.

Yoshara S. Barber

The Realness of the Illness

This illness was real without a doubt
Shadows of depression overtook the heart.
Fearful of new beginnings and where to start
Longing to find self, his world had fallen apart.

At one point he seemed to have it all
The career, a dream, he was standing tall.
In light of many he was shining through it all
Until one day, he never saw this downfall.

It was as if he had lost everything at once
Himself included, he put up many fronts.
Pretending to be okay, we all knew it could get worse
Not finding help rendered this generational curse.

He was mourning the death of a career
Lost of friendships and troubled fear.
Wondering why this was not the year
The year he accomplished and persevered.

Drowning in defeat, filled him with regrets
Suicidal thoughts, feelings of nothing left.
To end this life will be all better more
Reminiscing on the past and the way his life was before.

Why was this man afraid to ask for help?
Societal views that men don't cry for help.
Avoidance of the truth and empty scars
Trapped within his own prison bars.

A disbelief in God since life had took this turn
A turn for the worse and feelings of discern.
Regretful yet hopeful that this wasn't the end
Actual realizations that mental illness was real.

Cries in the darkness of how to release this hurt
Alone is lonely, no one was in his corner.
Prayers to the most high, releasing everyday struggles
What was next for him was working thru the troubles.

To find himself was most important
Focuses of what would push him further.
Granting himself permission to be better
Steps of faith improving for greater.

Now was the time to conquer a new start
One day at a time he felt it in his heart.
That today was the day to figure out his worth
And not hide the insecurity of this rebirth.

"You are not a victim. No matter what you have been through, you're still here. You may have been challenged, hurt, betrayed, beaten, and discouraged, but nothing has defeated you. You are still here! You have been delayed but not denied. You are not a victim, you are a victor. You have a history of victory."
Steve Maraboli

HER Defeats

She used to dream a lot, talk to herself, place herself in these fantasy settings because she knew that there was something better at the end of the tunnel. That although she couldn't grasp her mind around it because of the situations she was in, the belief that she envisioned better was enough. You see, during the tryout phase of our lives, we are fearful. And that fear residues from lack of self-confidence that we can have better or that better is for us. We must maintain a positive mindset despite our circumstances. If you have a positive attitude and constantly strive to give your best effort, eventually you will overcome your immediate problems and find you are ready for greater challenges. She told herself that she was prepared for whatever challenge despite her many failed attempts. Life was throwing her lemons, but she was prepared to make lemonade. She chose knowingly to tell herself stories that would uplift her circumstances rather than continue to drown in defeat or depression. She understood then that mental illness was real, and if not careful it would affect her even long after.

The reality is that at some point in life we all go through struggle, but we get to choose how we respond to it. We get to choose whether or not we allow that struggle to hinder us or to simply motivate us. The ways in which we identify our challenges is the first way in which we succeed. Believing you can achieve your goal provides the foundation in overcoming your challenge, but also making sure you have a plan to address any risks when they arise is important. During the tryout phase of our lives, it is critical to set goals and follow through on commitments. It is a lot similar to creating a bucket list and thoroughly creating vision boards for your life. In the book of Habakkuk 2:2, it states to "Write the vision and make it plain so that he may run that readeth it," meaning whatever comes to mind that you see forth in accomplishing, write it down, pray on it, and if your plans align with God's then it's sure to come to pass. Regardless of your circumstances or past failures, don't allow a failed attempt to cause you from attempting another solution. Delayed doesn't necessarily mean denied.

The goals she set for herself were accomplished because she changed her mindset. She did not allow the lack thereof to affect her but rather motivate her to achieve greater things. Goal-setting is relatively simple if you follow a few simple rules. A goal should be challenging but achievable. It is important that you establish your goals at the beginning and make sure they are outside your comfort zone (Don't set your sights low). In addition, make sure the goal is measurable so you can monitor your progress on a regular basis. And most importantly, celebrate success. This is exceptionally important.

Rebirthed

The start of a life as a physically-separate being
The process of bearing or bringing forth an offspring.
This child that I carried I had not known what it would mean
To raise them through life until they were eighteen.

Rejected before birth they had no clue
What it would be like to even subdue.
The circumstances, trials just trying to make it through
Isolated fears, ready for a breakthrough.

My worst critic in that I felt so embarrassed
For my child, who was neglected by one of his parents,
Unknowingly lost that this wasn't the fairest
Producing unhealthy fruits because they were careless.

Church folks frowned upon my indecisions
Blinded by circumstances and insecure conditions.
Faulty to my beliefs because these were their religions
Shunning me out unaware of my provisions.

Timeless efforts to work through this grief
Pushing my way forward for better relief.
Finding new outlets so I could release
Release shameless guilts in efforts to proceed.

For they were the rebirth I had not understood
And all they needed was a chance to feel secured.
Secured in love instead of feeling misunderstood
A chance to feel complete regardless of what occurred.

Yoshara S. Barber

My children, I'm thankful that you chose me
Without you two who knows where I would be.
Lost in a world, still trying to find me
Running from pains caused, still trying to be set free.

Who knew your births would grant me a chance to be reborn
A chance to live freely a chance to be transformed?
In a society that judges us for everything that we've done
Understanding your purpose meant understanding this outcome.

For God said no children are a mistake
Regardless of fears and troubled heartaches.
Permission to move forward was just what we needed
Forgiveness of neglect and how they were treated.

Experiencing rebirth in terms of being reborn
That season of devastation was what I needed to reform.
Reform back to God's faithfulness and love for our lives
In an effort toward changing and willingness to survive.

"Behold, children are a gift of the Lord,
The fruit of the womb is a reward."
Psalms 127:3

HER Reawakening

She was the young woman who eventually became her worst critic because in society's eyes, the choices she had made were wrong. We live in a world where people are so judgmental, and the decisions we make are depicted by our flaws. Our characters are ripped apart and our integrity is shamed. We soon face challenges and unaware struggles because we do not understand how a single two-word phrase of "I'm pregnant" can hold such a negative perspective to some men. She questioned how the fathers she chose for her children were a mirroring image of the father she despised at one point in life. The man she was running from because of his past choices, was now like the exact same men she had chosen for her children. Men who were broken, who she didn't realize were broken at the time, but who each shared similar things in common.

Although God saw their children as a blessing, they saw differently because of their circumstances. In the beginning, the blessing itself was missed because now the issue was a divided opinion on parenting. The main issues stemmed from two individuals who were brought up differently and now projecting those same differences on to one another. Feelings have weakened because what was once a temporary fix is now the same fixation that is placed upon your child, which is temporary time. The time that you once shared is now decreased because in reality, no one was ready. No one was ready to agree on the proper welfare of the child because that alone would involve a lifetime commitment. And so now there are disputes on financial stability for the child and whether a particular item was deemed appropriate or not. Isn't it something how we become so ashamed of the process that we don't feel we can survive the delivery?

She learned to figure out how to see the blessing in the situation. Each day she prayed and asked God to forgive her for the choices she made not realizing that this was all a part of His plans for her life. It was in fact the first realization she had, that she didn't choose this life but rather it chose her. God chose her children as blessings for her, but for so long she couldn't see that because she was blinded by circumstances. The struggles she saw it as were merely a blessing in disguise.

What if the love that is shown toward your child is the only love they had known? What if that was how their fathers portrayed love and that is all they know? I learned that we cannot take it personal regardless of how much it hurts. People often show affection based on what they have known in that moment, and it isn't until they have healed themselves and have acquired the knowledge it takes to be better, that they find out who they really are capable of becoming. Don't take it personal. Heal what is broken in yourself. Forgive those for your peace of better understanding and continue being the best parent you can be.

So, What Are You Producing?

You see, when you are birthing something, when there is something growing on the inside of you, it takes all of you to bring it to life. And during the rebirth process, you have two choices. You can either allow yourself to become easily accessible and acceptable, or you can require yourself to grow. She spoke to herself daily saying that she would no longer feel ashamed because life didn't go how she planned, and so I ask, what are you producing? It is easy to live in the comfort of a world that you created, but are you producing good fruits? We spoke metaphorically of her children being her rebirths, the reawakening she needed and that they were what inspired her to choose to produce healthier habits and a better lifestyle. God knows what you are silently carrying. Take a moment to be thankful for all the things that were not a part of your plans, and begin to assess those things you are birthing in your life. Now, allow them to be your motivation for change.

Yoshara S. Barber

Prison of Peace

I was trapped in the darkness of a prison
Prisoner to my own beliefs.
I was backed in a corner, I was hidden
Ashamed, confession was the only release.

I didn't understand this prison
The bars locking me closed.
The lack thereof of my indecisions
Angry I was ready to explode.

At the time I had no idea that this prison was just a test
A test of my faith and my abilities, ability to reduce the stress.
Looking for peace in all the wrong places
Searching for comfort with unfamiliar faces.

He had locked me in this prison for a reason
Reasons I had not understood.
This was all just a temporary season
A season that was working for my good.

He said, "If you can't make do in this prison,
To work toward what you want,
Then how can I provide you with plenty,
My child, are you only looking to flaunt?"

With no serious hesitation, I was ready for what I was facing
In this cell I wanted peace, I was ready to embrace it.
For a lack of better judgement, it was best I do the time
The time I was acquitted for until it was my time to shine.

To understand that, this prison sentence wasn't long
A test of strength and agility to see if I belonged.
Removing the bars of brokenness, guilt, shame and defeat
Releasing the pain of regrets and feelings of incomplete.

This prison had granted me peace
And I was finally at a place of rest.
Understanding my purpose to increase
Ready to do my best.

So, I say don't be ashamed of the prison that you are in
For God loves us so much regardless of how your life has been.
Make do with what you have in the prison to find your inner peace
Focusing on moving forward, working toward your masterpiece.

For He cannot provide a palace
If you do not go through the prison gates
Advocating for yourself,
Motivated to release the dead weight.

"Today I choose life. Every morning when I wake up I can choose joy, happiness, negativity, pain ... To feel the freedom that comes from being able to continue to make mistakes and choices, today I choose to feel life, not to deny my humanity but embrace it."
Kevyn Aucoin

HER Choices

She recalled listening to a message from the inspirational Oprah Winfrey, and she was particularly speaking about successes and how much you need your losses just as much as you do your wins because it is in your failures in which you succeed. That your failures are just there to point you in a different direction. And one of the things that stuck with her was when she stated, "Ask yourself what the next right move is?"

She recalled having many dreams and goals of becoming a published author, a motivational speaker, and to one day have her own nonprofit organization. She remembers writing those goals and aspirations down. Each day she would pray that her dreams would eventually become her reality, but she remembers not knowing how to take the first step toward accomplishing those goals. She encountered so many obstacles and there were various hurdles that had to be crossed. She wanted success so badly, but she was unaware of the process that was necessary toward obtaining it. You see, to me she just wanted someone to simply tell her how to get it so that it could get done.

Do you ever feel that way? Like maybe your destiny seems so far away only because someone who already has it won't just tell you how they did it, so now you're stuck trying to figure it out on your own and your way seems to be a bit challenging and you feel trapped within your own prison. That is what appeared to be happening in her life.

In order to become successful and become a winner, one must first learn to work on building and sustaining healthy relationships. The most successful people have healthy relationships with others—first with God, then yourself and then with others, because this is what happens when you don't have a healthy relationship with God: You look for others to validate you. You look for others to make up for the hurts and the disappointments and to acknowledge that you are worthy of something. You are looking for approval, but if you had a relationship with God, you would already have known that you were worthy. You would have acknowledged your strengths even while hitting a few bumps in the road because the scripture clearly states that "I can do all things through Christ which strengthens me" (Philippians 4:13). You have to get to a place where you are so whole with producing healthy relationships, that leaving an unhealthy relationship won't affect you when they don't apologize for how they treated you.

Don't allow fear to stop you from pursuing your goals all because your life is not going how you planned. Get to a place where you can forgive those who have hurt you in hopes of receiving something even greater. We must remember that in wanting successes one must be willing to sacrifice because success requires sacrifice. Life requires so much from us. It requires being vulnerable. It requires being rejected, inadequacies and insecurities, but trust me, you have what it takes. Take a moment to relax through the process and simply choose from this point on what your next right move is. We are all struggling with something, but your life is bigger than any one moment. You have to believe that.

Yoshara S. Barber

Shadow of Emotions

Profound sadness is what they felt
Disbelief, emptiness, affections dwelt.
Guilts, regretful about things they didn't say or do
Shunning others out just trying to make it through.

Numbing the pain, refusing to show emotions
Surviving the thought of Mama and her many devotions.
Devoted to her family and close loved ones
Forgiving, understanding through struggling outcomes.

Their mother had passed and gone to higher places
Trying to find comfort in faith knowing there was no replacing.
Wondering why her, shocked with grief
Unwilling to let go to turn over this new leaf.

Angry at the ones He didn't take before her
Lost in the silence, a visionless blur.
Why my mother? The questions arose
Was there not another family you could have chose?

To think that she won't be here to see me grow,
The many goals accomplished she'll never know.
The advice I kept from her in order to show
My children that the good Lord can bestow.

Hurting inside, I just want you to know
That I love you so much and I've been very low.
To the point of running and being solo
One more day in your presence I need you to show.

Their world was now turned upside down
Adjustments to life and many frowns.
Healing seemed like a lifetime to take
Sleepless nights and many headaches.

But they were willing to do whatever it would take
Regardless of pain, and troubled heartaches.
Relying on memories and various keepsakes
Remembering the good times trying not to break.

Breakdowns because their world felt so empty
Shadow of emotions ever since you left me.
Needing their mother's advice as the years went on
Struggling to stay afloat, since she was gone.

> "How could you go about choosing something that would hold the half of your heart you had to bury?"
> Jodi Picoult, Mercy

Why HER

Nothing can prepare you for what it's like to lose a mother. She had yet to experience it, but she sympathized with many friends who experienced the loss of their own mothers. At first she was unaware of how to comfort them when in fact, who they needed most was now gone. The biggest mistake was allowing herself to keep them busy. Although her intentions were pure in that she did not want them to break, she should have allowed them time to feel what they needed to feel in order to heal.

This situation was quite similar to Kanye West. In my opinion, Kanye kept busy to keep from truly grieving the loss of his mother, until one day he just broke. For many years she watched family members close to her keep busy at the loss of her grandmother, until one day they just broke because they pushed the grief away. They didn't want to allow themselves to feel the pain but rather ignore it. Grieving is a process and there is no time limit on how long that process should be. The more you push grief away the more it will find you. The focus should be on finding your peace when dealing with the loss of any parent, guardian, or someone close to you. People find comfort in different things. The important thing is not in what you do but rather finding something for you, something to help you move forward in an effort toward regaining peace. Do not allow anyone to diminish the moments that were meant for you to heal. At some point in your life, you will find the joy to smile again.

Coping with the loss of a loved one can be stressful and cause a major emotional crisis. It takes time to fully absorb the impact of a major loss. You never stop missing your loved one, but the pain eases over time and allows you to go on with your life. If someone you care about has lost a loved one, you can help them through the grieving process. Don't offer false comfort. It doesn't help the grieving person when you say, "It was for the best" or "You'll get over it in time." Instead, offer a simple expression of sorrow and take time to listen. Make yourself available to talk. Be patient and remember that it can take a long time to recover from a major loss.

There's nothing good that comes out of the death of someone you love, but she learned this: The magnitude of the pain you feel is a testament to the love you shared. And while you may never expect to arrive at a point in life where you are all right with the fact that your loved one is gone, soon you will realize how lucky you were to be loved and been loved that much by anyone.

Ultimate Sacrifices

The Daughter
Even at a young age is taught the fundamentals of how to properly care,
It is in her upbringing that she learns what it means to fully be aware.
The beginning of a major sacrifice is something she isn't prepared
The reality of her own family can leave her visually impaired.

She thinks she is ready because in her eyes she is able to create this ideal fantasy of the way her family should be,
When in actuality she is blindsided by what is yet foreseen.
She is ready to run to a place that feels safe—one in which she can call home,
Not knowing that the emotion would leave her feeling all alone.

The Woman
Being a woman meant understanding the various perspectives of the term womanhood
That even though society constitutes their own definition, the woman is often misunderstood.
She was forced to adapt to a society full of competing and comparing
A lesson in which she would soon find herself deeply regretting.
The world saw her as powerful; she wanted to be transparent
That strength in itself I believed was to me quite apparent.
She was ready to face adversities that may have come her way
A challenge that no one knew she would later learn to outweigh.
Outweigh the good from the bad, the rights from the wrongs
While learning how to adjust in a society she felt she didn't belong.
To the woman who possessed a strength no one could fathom
Not knowing that emotion would leave her saddened.

The Wife
Her role required being pleasing and satisfying to her spouse
Submitting herself was the ultimate cost.
50/50 had no room to play
It was 110 or more or there was no way.
The love she poured in he could never suffice
This had to be her ultimate sacrifice.
Pleasing and acceptable in every way imaginable
Trusting to his needs so that he could fully be pleased,
He learned to succeed.
Allowing him to be the head, so the family could be well cared,
In an effort toward being happy
An emotion that left her some days feeling crappy.

The Mother
The nurse, the teacher, a counselor—wrapped in one
Superwoman to her family, her work is never done.
An intangible glue that bonded like no other
The love she shows can be compared to no other.
Sensitive to the needs of many, her emotions can leave her feeling quite empty
Her heart is pure for they trust in her abilities.
The ability to protect and care for a life totally dependable
The blessing it seems can often leave her confused to face the unthinkable.
For an unconditional love her children gives is something she is grateful
Preparing them to take their toll in a world full of people who are often hateful.
Knowing you can't prevent them from pain or social injustice
Continuing to pray for those as they cry out just "trust us."
She is hopeful in knowing she has done her best
Relying on God's unchanging love despite the present tests.

The Sacrifice
All combined she realized her role
In a world that left her often feeling cold.
She was hopeless to the fact that she was just existing,
Existing in their world that often left her feeling empty.
She sacrificed everything for the reality she thoughtfully planned
For the family, the job and this life she had sustained.
To the ones she loved, that loved her for her many titles,
Often curious if any saw her as their idol.
Many days she felt like running
Thinking to herself no one would ever see this coming.
Pure hearted she was able
Not a selfish bone to be even capable.
This ultimate sacrifice was definitely worth it
But some days she wondered would they even notice
That all she wanted was for someone to take notice.
That these ultimate sacrifices were sometimes immeasurable
To the amount of times the world left her feeling vulnerable.
Just a need to feel appreciated in a world where she felt dictated
She found hope in knowing that although she had little worries,
    nothing compared to a family worth loving. **Her Sacrifice**

"The more I go through parenting, the more
I owe my parents an apology."
Unknown

HER Sacrifice

In the beginning when one first becomes a parent, they have a willingness to sacrifice their futures for their child's future. Having children, maintaining a family, or being a wife requires much sacrifice. It is said that women sacrifice more for their families, but that is neither here nor there. We aren't here to distinguish on whether or not men sacrifice more or if women do, but rather focus on how to get back to a place where they don't forget to take care of themselves also.

Children receive a lot in terms of parents working to meet their everyday needs. Parents sacrifice money, time with others, their careers and social life. She realized when her children were born that she had forgotten what it was like to take care of herself. In society's eyes, we are taught that taking care of self is somehow selfish when in fact it is the glue that keeps everything together. She had forgotten who she was because now they were the most important. What she learned was that in sacrificing so much to make sure everyone else around her was okay, she still did not need to forget about herself. What naturally happens is that once others forget to take care of themselves, they in return forget how to really take care of others. They become out of balance and that imbalance creates dysfunction.

To her children, she wanted them to know that she did whatever it took to give them her all. She worried often, failed at times, and she did not always get it right, but she tried her hardest even if it required sacrificing herself to give them the world. Lost in a society where she felt hopeless, she had every intention of being great—good and grand—but some days all she could be was okay. Her sacrifice for them was most important.

Rejection was the Set Up

When I mention the word rejection the room is always so still. It's one of those topics that becomes quite sensitive to the average person who hasn't quite healed. Most hear the word rejection and they run—running from fear and the pain it causes and the hurt that is still very present.

Take the little girl, for example, who longed for a relationship with her father. For a man to simply teach her how a woman should be treated, to love her like a man should love her. And to protect her like father is supposed to do.

But instead she received the "player dad" or maybe it was the dad who didn't like her mother so he couldn't fathom the thought of looking at her kind-of-dad. Hmmm … or was it the selfish dad? You know the dad that only thought of himself and any and everything that wasn't beneficial to that wasn't included.

Or could he have just been a deadbeat dad? You know the "I didn't sign up for this this year, but maybe next year" kind-of-dad." Or what about that kid that wasn't good enough for dad? The one who had other kids but this one wasn't right because he was too bright or was it the other way around?

I imagine the woman who was rejected so much that it became second nature to her. No one to ever show her how to love and how she should be loved. No one willing to stay around and break down the walls she continued to build out of fear, hurt, anger and defeat. I imagine how the rejection caused her to question herself, her sense of self-worth, and her value.

I imagined how the rejection pushed people away because she wasn't true, but to who? Did they really feel that after all the pain endured that she would have grown or she should have known?

This woman didn't have a clue. We are rejected in all areas of our lives. Whether I wanted to be in this relationship and he or she didn't choose me. Or you say you love me, right? But in society's eyes, I am a fool for loving you. I felt I deserved the promotion but the boss overlooked me. Or I wanted that job, but I was told someone else was more qualified for it. Why didn't my marriage work? I did everything right in my eyes, yet my best wasn't good enough.

How do we live through rejection from those who were supposed to cover us? From those who promised to always love us. Do you know what it feels like to love someone more than they love you because it's not reciprocated? Rejection hurts! Rejection hurts! And I'll say it again, rejection hurts!

That little girl suffered daddy issues because she was rejected from a father's love. And that little boy grew up hoping that he would eventually rise above, above the statistics of being yet another black man who was the product of a single parent household. But you see, they were still healing. They didn't realize that the rejection was the setup. That the rejection was the setup. That their rejections were a setup.

You see, GOD said, "I needed you to go through a season of rejection just so you could see your assignment." She had to understand that those who had rejected her were not over her, that they didn't control her, but that He needed her to be delivered from them so she could be set free and live peacefully!

The rejection was the setup because had she not been rejected, she would not have been able to handle her next assignment. She thanks God for those that rejected her and her kids, because the moment they got rid of her was the moment God placed His hands on her. That was the call of God over her life. Her rejections from man was an acceptance from God.

And it wasn't until she felt rejected that she figured out her value. And it wasn't until she felt rejected that she realized her worth. And it wasn't until she felt rejected that she understood she had choice in the matter. You see, through the rejection process, she was looking for a chance. She was looking for a chance for someone to commit, for someone to simply say you are it.

Last year she was waiting on a chance, but this year when she realized she had a choice in the matter, she was able to negotiate on her own terms. Rejection did that. Her prayer now is "Lord, only send me what I can handle because every option that I choose not only affects me, but my children as well."

She thanks God that something good came out of her bad experiences. She continuously thanked Him that something good came out of the rejections, and she was able to heal. She understood that her purpose was somehow worth the pain.

You see, when you can finally confront the very thing that tried to hurt you, that's when you can heal and speak about those things, and love the very people in spite of how they treated you. That is when you can heal. Trust the process, but in that, remember the setup.

> "We all learn lessons in life. Some stick, some don't. I have always learned more from rejection and failure than from acceptance and success."
> Henry Rollins

HER Rejections

There is probably no feeling worse than a feeling of being rejected. Whether you are rejected by a family member, a parent, a boss or someone from the opposite sex, the feeling you feel when your presence is denied or unwanted is indescribable. However, learning how to respond and understand why your rejections were needed is vital.

Rejection is sometimes never about who we are. It's often about someone else's inability to accept you for who and where you are. It hurts. But the process of rejection is there to guide you through life for a reason. The most common form of rejection comes from parents, while others come from the opposite sex. Regardless of who you are or what your truth may be, if someone has a fear of rejection they won't be able to accept your truth. The fear of being rejected allows one to feel incapable of expressing themselves and they lack a sense of personal identity.

Our rejections are a setup. Rejections are God's way of saying I have something better in store for you. Be patient. They are an opportunity with an understanding that delayed doesn't necessarily mean denied, that we need our nos just as much as we need our yeses. Do not fear rejection. You learn to accept "no" when you are working for something of a higher purpose. You realize how much you need the rejections in order to move forward. Understand that if you aren't being rejected, you aren't working hard enough. Get to a place in life where you can identify what you want and why it is important to you. Recognize the type of rejections you fear and learn how to work through them often.

It is important to focus on ways to improve yourself when dealing with rejections. It is equally important to learn how to build your confidence in such a way that you no longer concern yourself with whether or not someone will accept you. The more confidence you begin to build within yourself, the more others will begin to have in you.

Embedded Fears

Numbness which leaves you feeling depressed
Unwillingness to step out of comforts to face the tests.
Anxiety flares from deep within
The thought of obtaining more, shadowing new beginnings.

A leap of faith is what it would take
A jump of uncomfortableness in order to break.
Break away from embedded fears to reach your full potential
Breaking down the walls in efforts of becoming successful.

Because influential was who you were
But public speaking shattered the thoughts of obtaining more.
Or was it the thought of moving away,
Or a fear that you couldn't do the job the accurate way.

The fear that resided from deep within
Had over shattered her vision of how to begin.
Begin this new walk that required naming her fear
While rejecting its purpose, and the nervousness that appeared.

This would require a reconditioning of the mindset
Letting go of negative thoughts, challenging the aspects.
An action of commitment to suppress the nerves
Forgiving others also, and now focusing on what you deserve.

"You gain strength, courage, and confidence by every experience in which you really stop to look fear in the face. You are able to say to yourself, 'I lived through this horror. I can take the next thing that comes along.'"
Eleanor Roosevelt

HER Fears

The most common reasons people fear the resistance to change is fear of the unknown. We all want change and we want better things that come with that change, but the idea of what it takes to receive it we often fear. Fear is scary. Allowing yourself to step outside of your usual comfort zones is even scarier, but until you conquer and accept your fears you will never reach your full potential. If you continue to allow the encounters you face to disrupt your endless possibilities due to fear, you will never reach your full potential. You have to be willing to state what it is that you are fearful of and get to a place where you can overcome it.

She had plans of one day becoming a motivational speaker, but her fear was public speaking. She had plans of wanting to move to a new state that would provide her with more opportunities to support her family, but she was stuck within her own comfort zones. She had a fear at one point that better was not readily available to her. She didn't fear failure, in fact, it was quite the opposite. She was quite familiar with what failure looked and felt like. What she feared was success. She lacked the confidence that she could obtain greater because of fear.

You see, you must get to a place where you understand the process that comes with your defeats, but not be willing to conform to the belief that you aren't greater than what has already happened. Your past should never define you. You have to name what it is that you fear in order to reject the fear. It will require reconditioning your mindset in order to focus on the greater things that lie ahead. It will also require action to reduce what it is that you fear. Taking small approaches to recreate a new and improved you but this time with success.

You cannot change your community until you first change you. Do something every day that scares you, that scares the fear out of you. Fear cripples you. It can leave you feeling numb, but be willing to become uncomfortable at the risk of reaching your fullest potential by stepping out of what you fear.

When Broken Became Repaired

I was preparing myself for a healing,
Healing to become whole
My body ready to break and make amends,
To release this bondage of control.

This move toward wholeness
Was acceptable without limitations
It meant breaking down everything that wasn't you
To focus on greater expectations.

When broken became repaired
Was when I learned what it meant to completely heal
Heal the areas of brokenness
To obtain a love that was so real.

A love for myself
Because my purpose was somehow worth the pain
But this was such a pleasing pain
Used to help me regain.

Regain the strength to understand
How to heal from my broken wounds
And live a life that was fulfilling
Instead of prolonging with assumes.

Assumptions of emotions that ran deep
When relearning to trust,
Afflictions of my reality
Competent enough to readjust.

Learning from my experiences
I had to learn to trust
Trust that God would not fail me
Because moving ahead was a must.

It's always easy to remember
That life goes on regardless of the pain
Rejections and abuse
Try not to focus on the shame.

But instead, focus on ways
To heal for a better you
While changing up the dynamics
In an effort to pull through.

Because healing is so necessary
If you allow yourself the process
The process toward hope
A great and wonderful progress.

Loving yourself enough to believe
That the best was yet to come
Breaking the silence kept within
In order to become.

Become that greater individual
That you never knew existed
Effortlessly pursuing growth
Because now you were much more committed.

> "Healing takes courage, and we all have courage, even if we have to dig a little to find it."
> Tori Amos

HER Healing

The only person who can heal you is yourself. No one else can do it for you. It is a process you have to be capable of acquiring because it requires change. It requires courage. The courage to accept that your mother cannot heal you. The courage to accept that your doctor cannot heal you, nor your pastor. They can guide you along the way, and they can point you in the right direction, but the actual healing, the belief itself, lies within you.

Healing is the belief of what you are telling yourself. For example, let's just say you have a broken leg, metaphorically speaking, and the doctor gives you a cast. You don't realize that the cast is only there to help support the leg and keep the bones in tact, but what's happening on the inside? The actual healing has nothing to do with the cast, but many people would believe that the cast is what is actually healing them. Isn't it something that some people would rather still hold on to the cast to continue to gain sympathy for what's happening in their lives rather than remove the cast? Because that alone would require sacrifice. That alone entails fear and a strength which is buried deep within, and the thought of it seems too challenging to actually do something on their own.

That is the process of healing. We have become so complacent with holding on to the cast in our lives, rather than choosing to heal for greater purposes. Everything that you need already lies within you, but you have to believe it. No matter how much you pray, no matter how much you attend church or are fasting, if you do not have the belief that you will be better or that greater lies ahead, you will continue to fall short of the process.

Healing requires awareness, which is being aware of your endless capabilities. It is easy for someone to simply tell you to believe and to have faith, but if you don't understand what it means to actually acquire faith, how will you believe in it? You must be reawakened to who you are and who you are in Christ in order to heal, because our healing focuses on who we are. Healing is a state of being and once you realize who you are, in an effort to improve, everything else in your life flows the way it is intended. Trust the process.

For Better or For Growth

Everyone defines personal growth in his or her own terms
It's amazing how many people refer to it as a journey of lessons and concerns.

This courage to be greater requires more than just talk,
An act, a commitment, this was a brand new walk.

A walk through life to obtain growth and wealth
Success that required sacrifice, a life for better health.

Being better meant doing better, a chance to be great
A constant examination of having everything at stake.

An exploration of new ways to achieve a fulfilling life
The willingness and ability to make all things suffice.

Choosing not to make decisions based on fear and past experiences,
Embracing the process of spiritual and intellectual well beings.

Opening yourself up to the possibilities that you are capable of more
Reducing frustrations of negative energy and things you never asked for.

For better or for growth is not about becoming better
It's about recognizing who you already are and letting go to become greater.

Taking responsibility for your beliefs and things you have wanted
Learning about the benefits of personal growth that was granted.

This journey that in the end you will gain happiness and fulfillment
A real enjoyment that requires a lifetime commitment.

A commitment to loving yourself despite conflicts and sad endings
Being authentic and comfortable to embrace the new beginnings.

"Without continual growth and progress, such words as improvement, achievement, and success have no meaning."
Benjamin Franklin

HER Growth toward Progressing

She had to learn what it was like to reach her full potential, and that required self-growth. In order to progress and move forward, she had to set aside the weaknesses and focus on improving in other aspects of her life. We all need self-growth to improve in the areas of our lives. It is a desire to become a better you—not just a better you, but a greater you. That despite past failures you now have the ability to push through, regain strength, and become a refreshed version of yourself.

Greatness exists in all of us, but oftentimes we don't see it because we are too focused on others' successes around us. We become discouraged and do not believe that we are capable of those same successes. We make it more complex than it should really be. You must make a conscious decision and effort to be better each day. It requires dedication toward your goals. It requires perseverance and the willingness to craft your skill in order to progress. With self-growth comes understanding your personal development. It requires releasing the guilt, shames, and blames. Too often we would rather hold on to blaming our family members for the way our life turned out. We blame our bosses for the way our job is and oftentimes we blame ourselves for allowing so much ineffective change. But in order to become a better you, one must learn to do something different. What happened has already happened, but it doesn't change what can happen.

Self-growth for progression requires doing something different. It means focusing on what is going to move you forward. Learn to set small goals for yourself such as focusing on reading a book, working out, going for a walk, or taking a cooking class. Anything that you enjoy doing, whether big or small, that helps to improve your mind and functioning. Sometimes we cannot change the circumstance. The circumstance has already happened, however, we simply learn to adjust and rather focus on changing ourselves instead.

I Choose ME

I was trapped in a mind battle between who I wanted to be and who they reminded me I was
Wondering why it had to be that way or was this just because.
Because they only saw me for the shame I dealt with in my past,
Because there was a part of me that knew I didn't want the pain to last.

For I sometimes saw myself the same way they saw me,
And I knew in order to get to a better place this was for sure, unhealthy.
But my mind was telling me that my past was quite relevant,
And the other side of me wanted to focus on my developments.

I had to figure out how to take care of me first,
Not for the way they saw me, but the inner me I had grown to trust.
At the detriment of my own sanity it was best to let go
Of the people who were holding me back and reminding me, I would never grow.

Grow past their beliefs that a better life lied ahead
While releasing shameful guilt's and focusing on my improvements instead.
For this mind battle between myself felt so real
At one point believing their words, and the way they made me feel.

But at the risk of obtaining my destiny, I had to find my self-worth
Understanding my purpose and value, understanding this rebirth.
For I learned to recondition my mindset for my own beliefs,
And I learned to love the aspects of myself in an effort to release.

Release the people that were not supportive of my goals to obtain more
Release their negative energy as I should have done before.
I was broken but ready to be repaired. I had found a new love
Not your ordinary love story, but the love that allowed me to rise above.

Above their convictions and judgmental statements
Above their thoughts and reckless displacements.
For a healthier and happier version of me, was what was best
Even if it required disappointing others and feelings suppressed.

Me vs. me was my past verses my future
Running from the past, ready to embrace this new adventure.
Adventures of self-worth, learning to take care of self, first
Adventures of a new reality to obtain this self-growth.

Your relationship with self sets the tone for any other relationship you will possess
So put yourself first never requiring anything less.
Release the mind battles you carry based on other perspectives
Building your self-confidence, focusing on new ways to be effective.

"Women must learn to find self-worth within themselves, not through others. It is important to carve out a place just for you."
Georgette Mosbacher

HER Self-worth

She spent far too much time in her life and career making sure everyone else around her was okay—most times at the detriment of her own success. A wise person once said, "If those people had to choose between you and themselves, they would choose themselves over and over again." She knew she could no longer carry certain situations and people, not at the detriment of her own—not anymore at least. As time went on, she learned who was willing to grow in her life and who was content with staying the same.

What if the very people you are holding on to are the only people you believe you have in your corner? What happens when your family sees so little in you that you begin to settle for what they tell you? When they judge you for speaking a particular way? When they judge you for obtaining a higher degree, a better job or better neighborhoods than you weren't used to growing up? Or what happens when they judge you for your past failures? Or when you are continuously working toward growth, but reminded daily of past choices you've made?

I spoke briefly in an earlier section of how oftentimes many people want to pick and choose which family they should have been born in. Or because you had this friendship for many years, and you realized it was a one-sided friendship, you now need to figure out how to let it go and free yourself in order to get closer to your destiny at the risk of finding your self-worth. She learned to love the aspects of herself based upon the people around her, based upon what they taught her. She built her own support system in an effort toward loving the parts of her that she didn't know could be loved. She had to recondition her mindset in an effort toward knowing that she could obtain love. She was broken, but she was ready to be repaired. She leaned on the very people who were in her corner for comfort and support, and she realized who was really there for her. She could no longer carry the dead weight of negativity in her life from those friendships and family because you see, when you don't know yourself or even your worth, you are telling others that you aren't deserving of anything positive. She had to let them go because she was much more valuable to them in finding herself first.

Oftentimes we want to show our family how things could be in a different light, but sometimes our family isn't ready for what we are. We want to rescue them from what they are used to in an effort toward showing them that better can be gained. When she realized that better wasn't being obtained and that she was only being drained, she knew it was time to let go and let go fast. She experienced a season of judgement because she was no longer willing to lose herself at the detriment of having nothing, at the detriment of not succeeding.

Brokenness became repaired when she finally learned to put herself first. You see, her idea of putting herself first in the beginning meant being selfish because that is what society has taught us for so long, that we are selfish if we take care of ourselves first. We want to make sure others around us feel loved and understood, but we forget to prioritize our own happiness. We forget that in loving others we can somehow love ourselves too. Putting herself first meant being better, physically, emotionally, and mentally. The best thing she could become for her loved ones was to become a healthier and a happier version of herself, even if that meant saying no to disappoint others. Your passion for giving is a great reason why people love you. What people might not see, though, is the self-neglect that too often hides within people who love to please others because they are seeking validation because of their lack of self-confidence.

Her happiness was important, but not just for herself, for her children as well. Being consumed with problems from others can cause a great deal of stress, but releasing those stressors can reduce worry and detrimental health issues in your future. Taking care of herself first meant learning to love who she was. It meant taking time out of her day to do things that she enjoyed, the things that made her happy, even if only for a few minutes. Sit down and figure out where you can begin to put yourself first by doing activities that you love. It is important. The most successful people have great relationships beginning with self, first.

This was the best gift she could have ever given herself because now she was breaking the silence of acceptance from others and she was dancing in love—not your ordinary love story where she found companionship—but the love she finally found within herself, self-love and her self-worth. She learned to love her, flaws and all. She was willing to fix what she didn't like about herself. She learned how to cope with being a single parent. She learned how to adjust with all the inadequacies in her life, and focus on what was going to move her forward. She learned to become more transparent in revealing her truths, and she was okay with them.

You see, you cannot enter the door of success by first trying to bring others with you. You may lose a few friendships and relationships, but the process is demanded in order to grow. She was willing to allow herself to become an inconvenience to others at the risk of their convictions, in order to love herself first. The relationship you have with yourself sets the tone for every other relationship you will ever have. Do not forget to take care of you first.

Dancing Through

I was ready to dance like no one was watching,
I was ready to break through
Finally ready to let my light shine
And leave the darkness in the rearview.

I was dancing in the middle of the fighting,
Dancing in the mist of the rain
I was dancing like this was my last dance
Because it was time to release this pain.

It was time I danced my way out of fear
Rejections and loss of hope
Understanding that this was important
Making my way to approach.

Approach a new stage of life, that required letting go
Of past hurts and failures, abandonments and so much more.
I was finally divorced
Yes, I had pushed my way through
Divorced from my past and fears
Refreshing feelings of brand new.

This breakthrough was something I hadn't experienced before
It was my dance of freedom and forever more.

At my lowest was where I found strength
I was dancing on my own terms
At my highest I found the inner beauty
I was no longer stressed with the concerns.

Yoshara S. Barber

This dance of peace was just what I needed
To fulfill my dreams and goals
To dance my way through adversities
Because God had saved my soul.

I had broken through what society said was bound to keep me down
I survived what was worst in my eyes because my faith had turned around.

> "There's about to be a shift in your life. Get ready for your blessing. You've been through enough and a breakthrough is on the way. Don't doubt it, just claim it."
> Unknown

HER Breakthrough

Do you find yourself seeking a water well like Moses? Sometimes we just need a break from it all. She realized that today was the time to receive her breakthrough. She had been through enough. She had suffered enough and today was her season for change. Breakthrough means moving forward. It is an understanding of what has happened in your life and why it has happened with the knowledge to now keep trying. Our breakthroughs happen when what you're seeking gets delivered to you. Instead of running, crawling, or walking, she chose to dance her way through the obstacles. She needed God to intervene in her life to remove the hurdles placed before her in order to obtain her destiny, in order to receive this breakthrough.

You see, what you have to remember is that your life isn't over. You just had a bad start. Our past speaks to what we used to be, but it does not define who we are. You have to be willing to take that same energy you spend saying, "What if" and use it for what you can do now. Your life will flow smoother. I'm not promising it will be easy, but I have faith it will get better.

Until you learn how to live a fearless life, you will never obtain your destiny for breakthrough or change. You must be willing to elevate yourself so high that you are willing to take the first step toward change. Taking the first step is vital because without the first step there is no process and without the process, there is no progress. You must be willing to take action to move in a new direction. After all that is pretty much what a breakthrough is—a chance to move forward. Taking the first step is important in reclaiming your new life because it is unlike any steps before. Your breakthrough will not happen unless you are willing to believe that you can obtain it.

Her faith was based on what would happen next—after the abuse, after the rejections, and after the fear. Her faith was a constant reminder that she could obtain better, that a breakthrough lies ahead. She was willing to rise above the barriers that kept her silent at the cost of obtaining her destiny. We have all had areas in our lives where we said we were going to do something or we wanted to achieve something, but then we find ourselves pulling back. The key to a breakthrough is finding new approaches that work, cultivating effective communication skills while developing new strategies to push yourself even harder. Make sure you are implementing new goals that focus on being a better you because holding on to past failures prevents breakthrough. Do not focus so much on the story that happened before, but instead, divorce it and begin to fall in love with your truths.

United We Stand

We are women
Yes, we are strong you see,
Bridging the gaps between where we are, and where we'd hope to be.

We are women
Standing tall through the falls
The mothers to our children, the ones who risk it all.

We are natural leaders,
But they say not
Who else can balance professional and personal
Have they now forgot?

The many hats we wear to stay afloat
Pivoting, adjusting to solutions we must note.
Decision makers when dealing with a crisis
Passionate toward others to prove our sacrifices.

Those gender inequalities are something we're looking to break
Breaking into more roles that requires just a little shake.
Shaking hierarchies to demand that we are here
Here to stay so fear not. No one can stop what we've got.

Motivated by challenges, a strength not many posses
Stumbling upon obstacles in spite of feeling distress.
Fighting to belong in a world that favors men
Overcoming this stigma, a journey we're ready to begin.

We are women and we won't stop
We are the leaders of today's society
Have they now forgot?

There is an imbalance of who is in power because of the shortage of women this country required
Required to be in corporate roles, because they felt women could not handle the control
Control they believed our counterparts possessed, oppose to allowing us more opportunities instead of believing that we were less.

Motivated by success, we strive in all efforts to do our best
We are the glue that holds this country together
We are the ones who make it all the greater.

With confidence we are empowered to achieve
Efficient in our tactics we have the faith to believe.
Believe that we will soon have more women who are leaders
A breakthrough of gender equality, we are today's keepers.

Keepers and teachers who attribute to each other's success
This overwhelming freedom has all been just a test.
A test to see if we were ready for the fight
A fight to remove the social injustices that continue pulling us to new heights.

Showing society that women can conquer
Bridging communities to prove that we are just as stronger.
Providing unique measures to stand as one
United in all elements in order to overcome.

I am a woman
I know discrimination
I know what it's like to be underestimated
I know what it's like to face failures.

But you see, I am a woman who can handle it all
The critics, the bias decisions, the weight of it all.
Because United We Stand or divided we fall
It's in our duty that we not miss this call.

Our superpower is in being a woman
That despite the adversities, this woman remains humble
An act of true humility, resilience of a known leader
Ready for what was yet to come
Ready to face the unknown
We are women and today we belong!

> "A leader is one who knows the way, goes
> the way, and shows the way."
> John C. Maxwell

HER Leadership

Now was her time to exemplify the courage of leadership—not just any type of leadership, but women in leadership—women empowerment. This was the moment to break through social injustices and social inequalities and show the world that women have a voice too.

Women face challenges every day, but yet their strengths in being mothers and wives allows them to keep it all together. Every day we are forced to compete against our counterparts and remain underrepresented in the field. Women seem to be held to higher standards than men and often have to prove themselves more, but just like men, women want a seat at the table, too. She was finally at a place where she could focus on the aspects of her life that would move her forward. She had broken through many barriers and soon began to accept the weight of who she was. She was okay with who she was, but that now meant focusing on a way to be a better her in terms of leadership and seeing her successes.

This is to all the women who are single mothers and experiencing hardships; to the wives who are still trying to find themselves, and to the daughters who are seeking to find their voices. You have the ability to pursue your dreams—one stepping stone at a time, one day at a time. Had it not been for the stones thrown at her daily, she would not have been capable of building a bridge that would mend the brokenness of a society divided. Despite various circumstances, she was now the first in her family to obtain a college degree. She focused on youth mentoring within her community, building support groups to encourage other honestly broken individuals, volunteering within her local community, and she was accepted into the master's program for public administration. Besides that, she was writing her story.

You see, the challenges that we face are only there to steer us in a different direction. Maybe the path you are on doesn't seem to be the right one because you're continuously going left. Maybe you are stuck between where you are and where you want to be because your reality is causing you to become distrustful of the future. And what if your family is waiting for you to see what leadership looks like? That despite you falling short of the process of what has already happened, maybe you were put on this earth to show them a different way.

Leadership has nothing to do with titles. It has nothing to do with your personal attributes, and it has nothing to do with management. Leadership is the ability to improve at your capacity, putting your vision into reality. Leadership requires leading people and having followers while doing so. Her leadership was her ability to show the world that through self-determination you can possess the attributes of becoming a great leader. She could show her family that there were readily opportunities available if they were willing to take the first step and try. And she continued to prove to herself that she was capable of empowering a society that was crumbling, while conquering fears with the motivation to relive.

Epilogue

"She finally found her voice. Yes, she found what was hidden deep within. Beneath the scars, underneath the pain, she found what was missing."
Yoshara S. Barber

HER Silence Broken
(The Voice Within)

When you find your voice, you don't find some new thing inside you. Instead, you find a little more of you. You find a little more freedom to express and allow yourself to be heard. You find what's been missing. We have all suffered in some way with rejections, abuse, insecurities, loss of hope and brokenness. We've all had regrets, been fearful, and felt lonely. But in realizing she was hopeless, she found hope despite current circumstances. If it had not been for her rejections, she would not have been able to find her worth, and had it not been for the brokenness, she would not have found the healing within.

Her silence was broken and now her inner voice has spoken. The goal was in finding her purpose and strength. Her goal was to be happy because her happiness was important. Don't look to others to define who you are or what your purpose should be based on their perspective or their perceptions. Finding your voice means discovering the courage to walk in your own personal greatness. That although she saw herself as a writer, that was only one of the many ways that her story could be told. Throughout her life there were so many voices whispering in her head telling her, she wasn't enough; she was a failure, reminding her of all of her defeats and all of her wrongdoings. She had to find her purpose. And in finding her voice she was only able to do that through finding His voice—God's voice in listening to Him, in understanding the reason for each season in her life, in understanding His purpose for her life, and in trusting His plans for her life.

You see, in finding yourself you find out who you are. You learn how necessary your experiences were in order to heal. Realize that what happened in your life doesn't define what can happen with your life, that you can have a plan and purpose. Readjust the lens and focus on what is going right in your life. Trust that things will work the way they are intended for your benefit. Do not stress and worry about things you cannot control, and do not try and walk this path alone.

It is an incredible danger to live life without knowing who you are. How you process successes and failures in your life as they happen cultivates the ways in which you move forward. Your true self comes from your inner life. Learn to trust the sound of your voice, and listen to understand your intuitions in order to find your place of peace. Own your story. Own what has happened to you because once you accept your story, you now have the ability to rewrite the ending.

If you are willing to have a better life despite past hurts, daily struggles and fears, then you are on the right path to healing. HER Silence Broken Inspirations & Poetry is the inspiration for you. Conquering fears with a motivation to relive, the key to healing is in acknowledging everything that has happened in your life—the good, the bad, and the ugly—while focusing on rebuilding your self-confidence to produce a healthier life in order to obtain success.

HER Silence Broken Inspirations & Poetry provides detailed conflicts that many individuals have faced with little to no growth. This is the key to breaking the fears we've kept silent in an effort to reveal our hidden truths and accept who we really are in order to heal. Only we can take ownership in understanding the world we live in with an even greater purpose to accept ourselves and build lasting connections we can cultivate along the way.

About the Author

Yoshara S. Barber is a mother of two (Londyn and Carter), who currently lives in Jonesboro, Arkansas. She is a current graduate student at Arkansas State University, seeking a master's degree in public administration. She is a 2011 graduate of Arkansas State University, earning a bachelor of science degree in interdisciplinary studies with an emphasis in social work, education, and sociology. She is a hard worker who is committed to empowering women and changing the community around her. "In a society that allows you to become anything, I'm choosing to become a better me. Imagine HER."

–Yoshara S. Barber